Name Zacs

treats between me and Chas

nails trimming no clipper. Run around

Food 3 times a day on dry. Food

crate 2 hrs at a time leave home

Vac. in 3 weeks.

Door don't use front door.

Get Bully sticks

Heart warm spring.

Conservative on shots

test for worms - stool sample

Feed 10-2-6

When should I give canned
food? & Pumpkin

Day 1 1-6-2019
Fed at ? ½ cup
                              missed getting time
9:45 Pee & Poop
Bamp his head on door -no dossie door
missing his littlermates
Canned Food If bowels are runny
Part Canned Food Part Pumpkin 1 teaspoon
Fed 12:50

Fed bish Toke out Peed & Poof
Started marking.
1-7-2019
Took him out at 8 something
Fed when he came in
9:32 Went in Kennel and laid down

1-7-2019

Laid in sun spot.

Turned on nail grinder he came

over and just stood and looked at

it.

Took out 10ish peed & pooped

this was a

Came to me, put him in chair

with me 12:13 went to sleep

after chewing his hoove. Slept

until 1:50 took out feed.

Fed ate some not all of his

food at 2:15. Put in playpen to

relax.

Went on stool in winter to
laid down to sleep I put him
in his Kennel 3:30. Woke up at ?
Went outside and feed.
Fed at 5:50 he played very
little put in play pen he
laid down napped I got him
up at 6ish took him out, He
feed + pooped. Came in he
played some got in chair
with me chewed nylabone
in chair then went to sleep.
It is 7:56 and he is sleep.
Took him out around 9:32 +

Put him to bed at 9:52.
Hunkerd down in my chair
so I put him in his kennel.

1-8-2019 Tuesday

Woke up at 5:45 whining. Since he did not poop last night I figured he really had to go and he did. He came in ran around some I fed him. He came to me and looked like he needed a cuddle. Put him in the chair with me gave him some chews. That lasted a few minutes before he started to yawn and hunkered down. I decided to go ahead and put him in his kennel and come downstairs. 6:30 Chas + Tonto still up there sleep. Slept

until 11:15 took out peed.
Played until 12:05. Fed
him in his kennel.
Asleep at 12:55. Took him
out 3:00 feed + Pooped.
Fed him at 6:00.
Took him out at 7:00 to peed
+ poop afte playing. he did
both.

1-9-2019 Wednesday

Up at 6:45 goes outside to peed & pooped. Played until 8:10 crated. He was able to jump up on my chair while I was out of it. I am working on his name and sit comand. Up at 9:17. Played until 9:45 I fed him took outside until 10:10. He did pee & poop. Ran around the yard and seemed to have a good time running around. Came back inside played and chewed on Tonto's cheeks for a while in his cage and finally started to fall asleep. I put him in his kennel. He whined a little but settled down and went to sleep. 10:30. Woke up a few minutes later but after more play time he finally went back to sleep at 12:15. in the chair with me. I put him in his cage. Woke up 2:15 went outside peed. Fed at 2:25. Opened Tonto

Cage. Tonto growled. Zaccai sort of growled. Went out at 4:00 peed + pooped. He and Tonto almost played. They both did the bow for play and Tonto ran to porch. Zaccai wanted to go after him but needed to poop instead. Sleeping 4:50

1-10-2019 Thursday

Took out 7ish peed + pooped

Fed at 9:45 hunkered down

at 12:15. Fed at 1:45 hunkered

down at 2:15. Up and outside

at 4:15 peed + pooped.

Fed at 5:45.

1-11-2019 Friday

Taken Out at 7:00. Sleep at 9:14. Tried to train a little on walking on lead. Put up in our bed for first time he flipped and burrowed and sniffed. Fed at 10:50. He made it onto our bed by himself today. Poor Tonto he unknowingly showed him how to do it. Took out he peed. Fed at 3:25

1-12-2019 Saturday

Took 4:15 AM Peed + Pooped
Out again at 8:00 am
Peed + Pooped each time
he went out.
I did his nails as Chas held
him. He was so upset at me
that he screamed the first two
but turned his head and would
not even take treats from me
until it was over. I praised him
and he did take take treats.
Tonto is okay until he bites him.

1-13-2019 Sunday

Tish peed + pooped.

moved cage and play pen around.

Sleep at 11:33

feed at 1:45

Ate at 1:55

1-16-2019 Wednesday

Today when I got home at 4:55 took both dogs and Tonto played with Zaccai for a bit. Zaccai did his body bamp. He wanted to go and play. Worked a little on stay

1-19-2019 Saturday

Zaccai has bit a hole in his bed. He knows "In the House" and "Upstairs". Working on "In The Cage".

Eating + pooping well. Has continued to mark things.

Sort of doing the humping thing

97684609R10069

Made in the USA
San Bernardino, CA
24 November 2018